The Inuit
A Proud People

Deborah Kent

Enslow Elementary
an imprint of
Enslow Publishers, Inc.
40 Industrial Road   PO Box 38
Box 398   Aldershot
Berkeley Heights, NJ 07922   Hants GU12 6BP
USA   UK
http://www.enslow.com

Enslow Elementary, an imprint of Enslow Publishers, Inc.

Enslow Elementary® is a registered trademark of Enslow Publishers, Inc.

Library of Congress Cataloging-in-Publication Data

Kent, Deborah.
    The Inuit : a proud people / Deborah Kent.
       p. cm. — (American Indians)
    Includes bibliographical references and index.
    ISBN 0-7660-2451-2
    1. Inuit—History—Juvenile literature. 2. Inuit—Social life and customs—Juvenile literature.
I. Title. II. Series. III. American Indians (Berkeley Heights, N.J.)
E99.E7K439 2005
971.9004'9712—dc22

2004016147

To Our Readers: We have done our best to make sure all Internet Addresses in this book were active and appropriate when we went to press. However, the author and the publisher have no control over and assume no liability for the material available on those Internet sites or on other Web sites they may link to. Any comments or suggestions can be sent by e-mail to comments@enslow.com or to the address on the back cover.

Illustration Credits: Associated Press, AP, p. 42; Atlas of Canada, p. 43; © Corel Corporation pp. 1(left and center), 4, 5, 6, 9 (top), 12 (inset), 14, 15, 16, 19, 20 (bottom), 21, 23, 24, 25, 31 (bottom), 41, 44, 47; © Eastcott/Momatiuk/The Image Works, p. 29; Enslow Publishers, Inc., p. 7; Getty Images, pp. 37, 38 (top), 39; Hemera Technologies, Inc., p. 20 (top); © Hrana Janto, p. 26; Library of Congress, Prints and Photographs Division, pp. 9 (bottom), 28, 35; © Marilyn "Angel" Wynn/Nativestock.com, pp. 1 (right), 12, 30, 31 (top), 32, 33; National Marine Fisheries Service, p. 22; NWT Archives, pp. 1 (background), 13, 17, 24, 38 (bottom); Photos.com, p. 27; U.S. Fish and Wildlife Service, pp. 18, 34; Werner Forman/Art Resource, NY, p. 8.

Cover Illustration: © Corel Corporation (left and center); © Marilyn "Angel" Wynn/Nativestock.com (right); NWT Archives (background).

Contents

Two young Inuit women take a break from sledding with their dogs.

People of the Far North

The Inuit are a people of the Far North. The Algonquin Indians of eastern Canada called them the Eskimo, which means "eaters of raw flesh." Some non-Inuit still use this name, but the Inuit do not like it. The name "Inuit" means "the people" in Inuktitut, the Inuit language.

The land of the Inuit is cold and harsh. The Inuit learned to make the most of their scarce resources. Before the arrival of Europeans, they lived by hunting and fishing. Today most Inuit have chosen a more modern way of life. At the same time, they continue to honor their ancient traditions.

chapter one

The Land

Most of the Inuit live throughout a large northern area called the Arctic region. This area lies between the Arctic Circle and the North Pole. Some live in Siberia, which is part of Russia. Others live in Alaska, Canada, and Greenland.

The Arctic is one of the harshest regions on earth. Winter temperatures often drop to 45° F below zero. Even in the summer months, the ground only thaws a few inches down. Trees cannot grow in Arctic temperatures. The land is like an immense northern desert, covered with snow instead of sand.

The Inuit Then

In the past, most Inuit lived along the shores of Arctic seas. Others lived inland, far away

An Inuit hunter looks very small next to this giant iceberg.

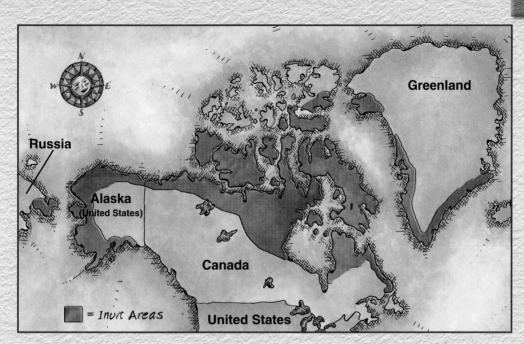

Map labels: Greenland, Russia, Alaska (United States), Canada, United States

= Inuit Areas

from the water. Wherever they lived, the Inuit faced the cruelty of the Arctic region. Freezing temperatures and starvation were constant dangers.

This map of present-day North America shows the areas where the Inuit lived during the 1700s.

The Inuit Today

Most Inuit still live in the Arctic. Many have moved to cities and towns. Today about twenty-five thousand Inuit live in Alaska. There are some forty thousand Inuit in Greenland and twenty thousand in Canada. A few Inuit have left the Arctic region for cities in a gentler climate farther south.

chapter two

History

The Inuit come from ancient Asian peoples. Small bands of wandering hunters moved from Siberia to Alaska about four thousand years ago. Gradually their culture spread eastward across the vast North American Arctic region.

These ancient people left behind tools that give clues about their way of life. They used whale oil to produce heat and light, burning it in limestone lamps. They carved knives from the ivory of walrus tusks. Such knives were shaped for cutting blocks of snow. These blocks

This is a special tool called a snow knife. These knives were used to cut hard, icy snow to make igloo houses. This snow knife is made out of ivory.

could be piled up to build a snow house, or igloo.

The Inuit survived mostly by hunting. They were nomads— people who did not stay for a long time in one place. They followed the caribou, seals, and other animals they used for food.

The Inuit are great hunters. This man hunts with a harpoon.

In about the year 1000, Norse settlers from Scandinavia in Northern Europe arrived on the coast of Greenland. They were the first Europeans to meet the Inuit. In 1576, a sea captain named Martin Frobisher set off from England. Frobisher and his

The Vikings came to Greenland in ships. They were the first Europeans to meet the Inuit. This ship's front is in the shape of a dragon head.

three ships reached Baffin Island in present-day Canada. The Frobisher expedition claimed the land for the English throne. At that time, there were probably about fifty thousand Inuit in the entire Arctic region.

Frobisher's men captured three Inuit. They took them back to England and introduced them to the English people. The English were amazed to see the Inuit man shoot ducks with arrows. He was very skillful and never missed. One eyewitness wrote that the Inuit were "very sharp-witted." He noted that they were "friendly and kind-hearted one to the other."

Mid 1800s: European fur traders explore the Arctic and trade with the Inuit.

1576: Martin Frobisher sails from England to Baffin Island; he takes three Inuit back to England.

1921: Knud Rasmussen studies Inuit traditions in Central Canada.

2000 B.C.   1000 A.D.   1500   1600 1700 1800   1900 1910 1920

Ancestors of the Inuit enter present-day Alaska from Siberia.

Norse settlers from present-day Scandinavia reach Greenland; they are the first Europeans to meet the Inuit.

1909: Inuit guides accompany Robert Peary and Mathew Henson on their expedition to the North Pole.

1924: The Inuit of Alaska become U.S. citizens.

During the next three centuries, Europeans seldom visited the Inuit. Then, in the 1800s, white fur traders ventured into the Arctic region. They gave the Inuit metal knives, kettles, and guns. In exchange, the Inuit traded the furs of foxes, mink, and other animals. European goods made life easier for the Inuit. Little by little the Inuit put aside their old ways. By the 1970s, most Inuit lived in permanent settlements. They held jobs and sent their children to school. At the same time, they kept many of their traditions alive. They continue to think of themselves as a unique people.

1999: Nunavut officially becomes an Inuit homeland.

1960s: The Canadian and U.S. governments strongly encourage the Inuit to give up their nomadic life and settle in towns.

1930 1940 1950 1960 1970 1980 1990 2000

1993: The Canadian government agrees to set aside the Nunavut Territory as an Inuit homeland.

2003: Jordin Tootoo becomes the first Inuit to play in the National Hockey League.

❖ chapter three ❖

Homes

The Inuit built many kinds of houses. The type of house a family made depended on the season and the materials that could be found.

The Inuit Then

The igloo, or snow house, was often the winter home of the Inuit in the Canadian Arctic. An igloo was a dome-shaped structure made from blocks of snow. It was ten to

Buiding an igloo is hard work. However, once it is finished, it offers protection from the wind and cold.

An Inuit family sits inside their igloo in the 1930s. The walls are black from the smoke from their burning lamp.

fifteen feet across at the base. The typical Inuit family slept on couches made of snow and covered with furs. Heat from a whale-oil lamp kept the igloo warm inside. In fact, sometimes it got too hot. Then the walls and ceiling would start to melt.

During the summer, the Inuit often lived in tents. The tents were made from the skins of caribou and other animals. In Alaska and Greenland, the Inuit sometimes lived in huts. A hut could be made from stones, earth, and wood. Since trees do not grow in the Arctic land, the Inuit used pieces of wood that drifted ashore.

The Inuit Today

Today most Inuit live in wooden houses. They have electricity, running water, and central heating. Life is much more comfortable than it was in the past. Inuit grandparents love to tell of the days when they built houses out of snow.

chapter four

Clothing

To survive in the Arctic land, the Inuit need warm, waterproof clothing. Proper clothes make the difference between life and death.

The Inuit Then

Before white people came to the North, the Inuit made all of their clothes from animal skins. Sealskin and caribou hide were most often used. Several layers of skins were sewn together. The layers trapped heat inside and protected the wearer from the icy wind. Usually clothes were lined with fur on the inside for added warmth.

Inuit women and men dressed much the same. They wore boots, socks, pants, and mittens. They also

The fur on this boy's coat is keeping his face warm.

This woman sews caribou hides together.

wore a hooded coat. The hood of a woman's coat sometimes had room to carry a baby tucked inside. A fringe of fur at the edge of the hood helped shield the wearer from frostbite. One type of hooded coat was called a parka. Inuit boots, known as mukluks, usually had sealskin soles.

Most Inuit women were good at sewing. Before she started to sew a new garment, the woman cleaned and softened the hides she would use. With a scraper made of bone or walrus tusk, she rubbed the hide until it was

This Inuit woman hangs fancy mukluks out to dry.

smooth and clean. Then she softened the hide by chewing. After years of chewing tough caribou hides, a woman's teeth were worn down almost to the gums.

Clothing needed constant care. In the extreme cold, the skins could become brittle and cracked. Wet clothes were hung outside to dry. The moisture turned to frost, which could be beaten away with a short stick. The girls and women chewed the dry leather to make it soft again.

The Inuit Today

Today only the oldest Inuit women sew animal skins. Most Inuit buy their clothes from stores or catalogs.

When they go out in the cold, they bundle up in down jackets and woolen mittens. Yet some Inuit styles remain very much alive. They have been an important influence on cold-weather clothes used around the world. Warm store-bought coats with hoods look much like Inuit coats of old. Fur-lined boots with sturdy leather soles are still called mukluks.

Mukluks are still worn today.

chapter five

Food and Meals

For food, the Inuit once depended on the animals that lived around them. Meat was the most important part of the Inuit diet. Today, the Inuit can choose from a wide variety of tasty foods.

The Inuit Then

Seal, caribou, and polar bear meat were staple foods for the Inuit. The ptarmigan and other birds were prized for their tender meat. The ptarmigan is a bird about the size of a chicken. The Inuit also ate a great deal of fish. The Inuit often ate fish and meat without cooking it.

Ptarmigans have white feathers in the winter. In the summer, their feathers are brown and black.

An Inuit hunter pulls a seal out of a hole in the ice.

Whale and seal blubber were special treats for the Inuit. Blubber is a layer of fat beneath the animal's skin. The Inuit diet was very high in animal fats. The bodies of the Inuit needed to burn fat to stay warm in the icy climate.

During the short Arctic summer, the Inuit gathered wild berries. They picked leaves and grasses that could be boiled to make tea. Tea was always offered to visitors.

Because meat was so important, most Inuit men were hunters. Hunting seals required great patience. First the Inuit looked for a seal's breathing hole in the ice. Seals can

Berries are gathered by the Inuit.

swim a long way underwater, but they have to come up for air. The hunter crouched on the ice beside the breathing hole. He might wait for hours before a seal came to breathe. Then he struck the seal with a harpoon. The sharp blade of the harpoon was carved from walrus ivory. It was attached to the handle by a long cord made of hide. While the seal struggled, the hunter cut the breathing hole larger. Finally he dragged the seal up onto the ice.

Inuit who lived inland depended on the caribou for food. Inuit women and children chased the caribou into a lake or cornered them near

Many Inuit join together to hunt caribou.

a cliff. Then the hunters killed them with spears or bows and arrows.

The Inuit Today

Today the Inuit get most of their food from stores and supermarkets. They enjoy the same foods that are eaten by most people in the United States. In addition, the Inuit still like fresh meat and fish. For many Inuit, wild game is still an important source of food. Now they hunt with rifles and go fishing in motorboats.

This man just caught a lot of fish. Both salmon and cod are fish that are common in the Arctic waters.

Some modern Inuit now use guns to hunt seal.

chapter six

Family Life

The Inuit have always had very close-knit families.
Cooperation was vital for survival in the Arctic land.

The Inuit Then

In a hut, tent, or igloo, Inuit families lived at very close quarters. No one had a room to himself or herself. Members of an Inuit family learned to get along without arguing or fighting.

Inuit children were very much loved. Children of two or three seldom heard the word "No." Everyone showered them with treats and attention. As a child grew older, he or she was expected to take on chores. Girls scraped and softened caribou hides. Boys learned

Kayaks were used for hunting. Inuit fathers taught their boys how to hunt.

to hunt. In the summer, boys and girls gathered berries. They collected eggs from the nests of gulls and other Arctic birds.

Adoption was very common among the Inuit. If a couple had no children, they might adopt the child of a neighbor with a large family. Adopted children usually stayed in touch with their birth parents. They grew up belonging to both families.

The Inuit Today

Today Inuit children watch television, go to school, and play video games. Yet Inuit families remain very close. Relatives are very loyal and try to cooperate with one another.

Grandparents are an important part of the Inuit family.

chapter seven

Everyday Life

The Arctic region is sometimes called the Land of the Midnight Sun. There, the sun shines for six months a year. During the other six months, the sun disappears and the land lies mostly in darkness.

The Inuit Then

During the dark winter months, the Inuit spent much time in their huts or igloos. They slept a lot to conserve energy. When the sun appeared, everyone became active. People went outdoors to work and play.

The Inuit used a boat called an umiak when they traveled by water. An umiak was a large boat made of skins. It

The sun shines even at night during an Arctic summer.

could seat a whole family. For hunting whales, they used a smaller boat called a kayak. On land the Inuit traveled by dogsled. The sled was made of driftwood or whalebone. A team of four to six dogs, called huskies, pulled the sled. The strongest dog became the leader.

The Inuit Today

Today the Inuit have clocks and electric lighting. They live by the twenty-four-hour day, like their neighbors to the south. During the sunny summer months, they still enjoy working and playing outdoors.

This dog team is battling through an Arctic windstorm.

chapter eight

Religion and Medicine

In the past, the Inuit believed that many spirits inhabited the world. Today, most Inuit are Christians. They still have a deep respect for the natural world and its creatures.

The Inuit Then

At the bottom of the sea, the Inuit believed, lived a powerful being called Sedna. Sedna was half woman and half fish or seal. If she was happy, Sedna sent fish and animals to the Inuit. If she was angry, food became very scarce.

Sedna was a very important goddess. The Inuit thought she controlled whether or not they could find food.

A shaman would often wear a colorful mask.

To learn why Sedna was angry, the Inuit would turn to a shaman for help. A shaman was a man or woman who could talk and listen to the spirits. Sometimes the shaman spoke with Sedna or other spirits in a dream. Sometimes he or she called to the spirits in a song. Inuit shamans also used special ceremonies to contact the spirits. After the song or ceremony, the shaman explained why Sedna was angry. The Inuit tried to make her happy again so the game would return.

The Inuit believed that spirits lived in every part of the natural world. The sky, the earth, the sun, and the caribou each had a spirit of their own. The spirits of people who died lived on among the Inuit. The spirit of a dead mother or father could give help and protection. The spirit of an enemy could cause sickness and trouble.

In this photo from the early twentieth century, an Alaskan shaman is trying to heal a sick boy.

If an Inuit was sick, a shaman might try to heal him or her. The shaman would ask the spirits what caused the illness. Maybe the spirit of an enemy was making a woman sick. Maybe she had offended the spirits by breaking an important rule. The shaman explained the cause of the illness. Then he performed a ceremony to bring the sick person back to health.

Missionaries began visiting the Inuit in the nineteenth century. They wanted to lead the Inuit to Christian beliefs. They discouraged their belief in spirits and their faith in shamans. Russian missionaries reached the Inuit of Siberia and parts of Alaska. They persuaded many Inuit to join the Russian Orthodox

Church. Protestant and Roman Catholic missionaries visited the Inuit throughout the North. They set up churches, schools, and hospitals.

Shamans nearly disappeared from Inuit life.

The Inuit Today

Today most of the Inuit are Christians. Yet they still find spiritual meaning in nature. One Inuit woman explains, "When I'm alone on a hill, I look at the distance and I see the beauty of the land, the water, the sky, and it's saying to me, 'I give you all this to enjoy.'"

This Inuit woman and her granddaughter attend a service at a Christian church.

chapter nine

Arts and Music

In the harsh world of the Inuit, nearly everything the Inuit made served a practical purpose. Yet the Inuit designed their tools to be beautiful as well as useful. Their love of beauty remains very much alive today.

The Inuit Then

Inuit with artistic talent brought out beauty in everyday tools. The shaft of a harpoon might be carved with figures of seals and whales. Carvings decorated the bone handles of scrapers. Hunters carried small carvings of seals, caribou, and other animals as good-luck charms.

The Inuit also carved masks of good and bad spirits. Masks were carved from whalebone or driftwood. Shamans wore carved masks during ceremonies.

This simple scraper was made from ivory.

Women sometimes wore small wooden masks when they danced.

Music was a very important part of Inuit life. Shamans sang special songs to the spirits. Women sang their children to sleep. Some songs told stories. The Inuit sang of great hunters and journeys over the ice.

The Inuit Today

Today most young Inuit enjoy pop music. They listen to their favorite bands on CDs. Inuit artists still carve figures of animals, birds, and people. Instead of ivory they use a soft stone called soapstone. Most of the soapstone they use comes from Quebec, Canada. The Inuit sell their carvings to tourists and art collectors.

Today, Inuit art is sold to tourists and art collectors.

chapter ten

Sports and Games

The Inuit are a fun-loving people. Recreation has always been an important part of Inuit life.

The Inuit Then

When storms raged, the Inuit stayed safe in their huts or igloos. During the long days indoors, they sang, told stories, and played games. Toys were carved from ivory or wood. Boys had toy harpoons, sleds, and bows and arrows. Girls had carved dolls and toy cooking pots. Girls also played with story knives. A story knife was a small blade for drawing on the snow. Girls drew pictures about the stories they told.

These boys practice the traditional Inuit sport of wrestling.

During the bright summer months, the Inuit played outdoors. Young men enjoyed fierce wrestling matches. Everyone played tug-of-war and games of skill. One game used a round piece of bone with holes in it. A player tossed the bone in the air and tried to catch it by putting a stick through one of the bone's holes.

When several Inuit families met, they often held a dance festival. They built a large igloo called a dance house. Drummers set the rhythm. The dancers often acted out a favorite story. Sometimes they wore funny masks and tried to make the spectators laugh.

This dancer wears a special outfit.

The Inuit Today

Today dances are still an important part of Inuit life. Families gather for dancing and storytelling as they did long ago. The Inuit also enjoy hunting and fishing as recreation. Some Inuit train dog teams for races over the snow.

chapter eleven

A Peaceful People

The Inuit valued cooperation more than fighting. They needed to work together in order to survive.

The Inuit Then

When two Inuit groups met, they usually exchanged a warm greeting. Next they shared whatever food they had. Delighted to make new friends, the children began to play. The grown-ups drank tea and talked.

Because life in the Arctic was so hard, the Inuit needed to help one another. They welcomed strangers and shared their scarce resources. When hunters killed a whale or walrus, all of their families shared the meat.

The Inuit people did not know what organized fighting was. Only rarely

Many Inuit join together to cut up a whale.

did one Inuit group attack another. Now and then, the Inuit fought with other peoples of the Far North. Clashes between the Inuit and other groups were usually brief.

Friends or relatives sometimes got angry at each other. On occasion, such arguments ended in murder. The victim's family would then kill the murderer or one of his relatives. The Inuit accepted such killing as justice.

Now and then, fighting broke out between the Inuit people and the Europeans and Americans. Most of the time, however, the Inuit welcomed traders and people called missionaries who tried to teach them about Christianity.

An Inuit and a fur trader make a deal at the Revillon Freres trading post in the early twentieth century. The trader is buying Arctic fox furs from the Inuit.

The Inuit Today

Though some Inuit today have joined the military, they are still mostly a friendly, peaceable people.

chapter twelve

Heroes

Inuit legends describe heroic hunters and travelers. Inuit heroes of today include artists and athletes.

The Inuit Then

Many Inuit legends tell about humans who fought animals or survived terrible storms. These legends were handed down from parents to children. They were told in the form of songs or long poems.

Great storytellers are famous among the Inuit. Their names may be remembered for hundreds of years. One storyteller was a shaman named Atsiluaq. Atsiluaq lived in present-day Labrador, Canada. Long before his people first saw white men, Atsiluaq told a strange story.

He said that some day men with white skins would come across the sea. They would carry a beautiful red cloth. Years later, white men arrived from the

Hudson's Bay Company to trade for furs. The Hudson's Bay Company flag was mostly red.

Many Inuit helped the white explorers who came to the Arctic. Robert Peary and Matthew Henson are usually thought to be the first humans who reached the North Pole. However, Peary and Henson did not reach the Pole alone. Their expedition included several Inuit guides. Among their most valuable guides were Inuit men named Utaaq, Ukkujaaq, Equinquah, and Sigluk. The Inuit knew the land and helped many explorers survive. Peary claimed the credit for himself. He wrote that the Inuit were not qualified to lead. He only admitted, that "they could drive dogs much better than any white man."

The brave Inuit explorers stand at the North Pole with another adventurer. From left to right: Ukkujaag, Utaag, African-American explorer Mathew Henson, Equinquah, and Sigluk.

In 1921, a Greenlander named Knud Rasmussen went

Knud Rasmussen was very good at speaking the Inuit language.

to live among the Inuit of central Canada. Rasmussen's mother was Inuit. He was fluent in both Danish and the Inuit language. Rasmussen studied the ways and legends of Inuit who had had little contact with the outside world. He wrote down their poems and legends. He described how they hunted, fished, and built their homes. Rasmussen's books are some of the best sources of information about traditional Inuit life.

Kiakshuk learned a valuable art before he died in 1966. Near the end of his life, Kiakshuk learned to draw. His drawings show Inuit hunts and dances. Many tell stories of the spirit world of Inuit legend.

Kiakshuk works on a copper engraving in a tent as an Inuit boy looks on.

Kiakshuk and other Inuit artists help preserve the traditions of their people.

The Inuit Today

Today many Inuit excel in competitive sports. In 2003, Jordin Tootoo signed on to play hockey with the Nashville Predators. Tootoo is the first Inuit to play in the National Hockey League. "When you see someone of your own make it, it makes it easier for the rest," said one Inuit leader. "This is the start of many."

Jordin Tootoo (right) battles for the puck against Tie Domi of the Toronto Maple Leafs.

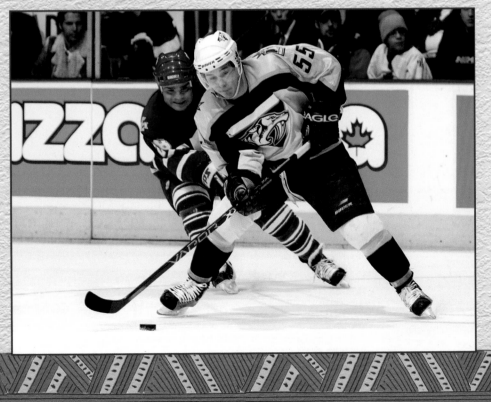

chapter thirteen

Government

In the past, the Inuit had no formal government. Today, they have formed organizations to address their concerns.

The Inuit Then

For the Inuit, the family was the most important organization. Months might pass before an Inuit saw anyone outside his or her family group. Sometimes several families gathered to hunt or perform a ceremony. After a while, they would scatter and go their separate ways again.

The Inuit were not divided into distinct tribes. However, the Inuit in various regions spoke different dialects. A dialect is not a separate language. However, it may have some unique words and speech patterns. Inuktitut, the Inuit language, has many dialects.

For thousands of years the Inuit had no chiefs or tribal councils. If a decision had to be made, the group turned to its most respected member. Usually this person was a shaman. Sometimes it was a hunter known for his skill. In the family unit, the father had the most power. The mother and the older children also spoke up, and their ideas were heard.

When white people came to the Arctic in large numbers, the Inuit needed to make bargains and treaties. As time passed, Inuit leaders began to emerge. They learned the ways of the whites. With this knowledge, they worked to educate their own people.

The U.S. and Canadian governments provided for the Inuit who lived within their borders. In the twentieth century, most Inuit began to live in towns and villages. They moved into houses built by the government.

In 1924, the Inuit of Alaska became citizens of the United States. For decades, Canadian Inuit sought control of their own land.

In 1993, Canada's Parliament approved the creation of an Inuit homeland. The Inuit homeland was

The Inuit sometimes turn to an elder for leadership.

officially established in 1999 and is called Nunavut, meaning "our land." It is a vast region almost as big as France. Nunavut was formerly part of Canada's Northwest Territory. Inuit make up about 85 percent of Nunavut's population. The capital of Nunavut is Iqaluit, the largest town. In Alaska, the Inuit have been given control of 12 percent of the publicly owned land.

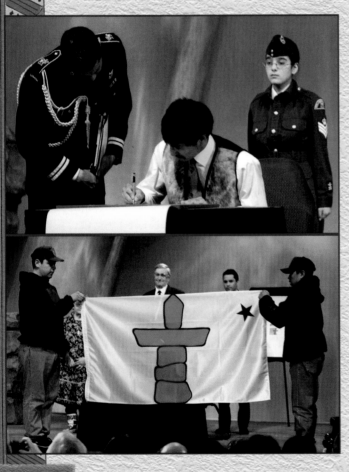

The Inuit Today

The Inuit are full citizens of the countries in which they live. Today Inuit in Canada and Alaska have the opportunity to govern themselves.

Nunavut's premier, Paul Okalik, signs a declaration that celebrates the creation of the territory (top). Two Inuit Junior Rangers show an audience the new Nunavut flag (bottom).

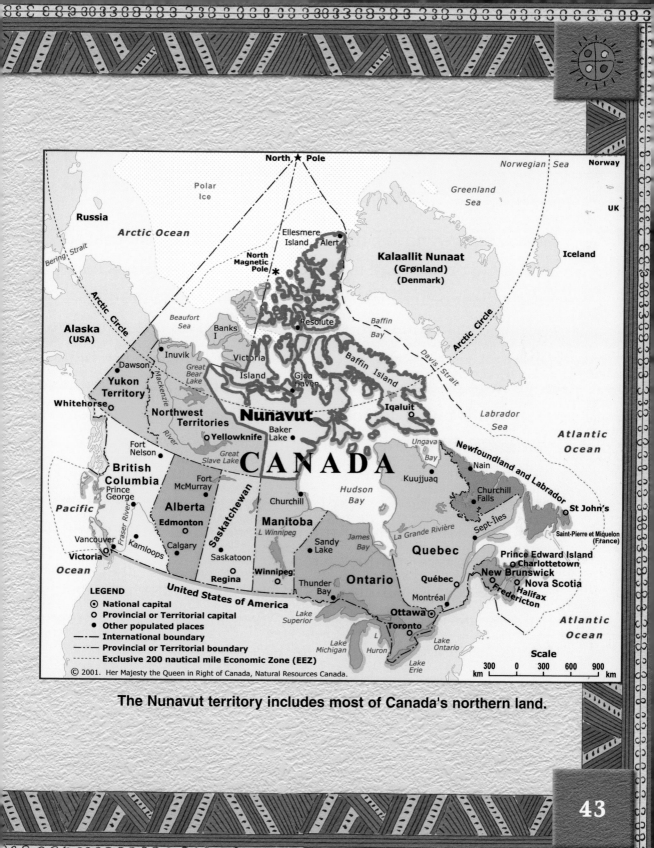

The Nunavut territory includes most of Canada's northern land.

Old Ways and New

Great changes have come to the Inuit. They have ceased to depend on the land for food and shelter. Dogsleds have nearly disappeared, replaced by cars and snowmobiles.

In the past, the Inuit struggled to survive. Life today is easier in many ways. Yet the Inuit are losing skills that once were prized. Young Inuit no longer learn to harpoon seals and build igloos. Instead, they study science, reading, English, math, and computers.

The Inuit welcome the improvement in education. However, they do not want their culture to vanish. They work to keep the Inuktitut language alive. Artists and storytellers record Inuit history.

In the past, the Inuit worked together to survive. Most Inuit today still remember that everyone benefits when people work together.

An inuit dog team makes its way across the Arctic.

Words to Know

amulet—A good luck charm.

caribou—A large animal in the deer family that lives in the Arctic.

culture—A way of life.

descended from—Are related to people that lived before.

dialect—The form of a language spoken in a particular region.

frostbite—The freezing of parts of the body which causes damage.

harpoon—A kind of spear used for hunting seals and whales.

husky—A sled dog.

kayak—A small boat once used by the Inuit for hunting.

missionary—Someone who goes to a distant land and tries to convert its people to a new religion.

nomad—Someone who moves from place to place and has no permanent home.

shaman—A person believed to have a special ability to communicate with the spirit world.

umiak—A large boat made of skins.

More Books!

Cordoba, Yasmine E. *Igloo*. Vero Beach, Fla.: Rourke, 2001.

Houston, James. *Tikta'liktak: An Inuit Eskimo Legend*. New York: Harcourt Brace, 1990.

Lassieur, Allison. *The Inuit*. Mankato, Minn.: Bridgestone, 2001.

Philip, Neil and Maryclare Foa. *Songs Are My Thoughts: Poems of the Inuit*. New York: Orchard Books, 1995.

Santella, Andrew. *The Inuit*. Danbury, Conn.: Children's Press, 2001.

Sharp, Anne W. *The Inuit*. San Diego: Lucent, 2002.

Williams, Suzanne M. *The Inuit*. New York: Franklin Watts, 2003.

Internet Addresses

Canadian Arctic Profiles: Indigenous People

<http://collections.ic.gc.ca/arctic/inuit/
people.htm>

Inuit Games

<http://gamesmuseum.uwaterloo.ca/vexhibit/
inuit/english/inuit.html>

Writing in Inuktitut

<http://www.halfmoon.org/inuit.html>

Index